DATE DUE			
OCT 1 0 1995			

CIRCUS STARS

THE PERFORMERS

Kyle Carter

The Rourke Press, Inc.
Vero Beach, Florida 32964

Edited by Sandra A. Robinson

PHOTO CREDITS
© Lynn M. Stone: cover, title page, pages 8, 12, 13, 15, 17, 18;
courtesy of Clyde Beatty-Cole Brothers Circus: pages 4, 7; courtesy
of Circus World Museum, Baraboo, WI: pages 10, 21

Library of Congress Cataloging-in-Publication Data

Carter, Kyle, 1949-
    Circus stars / Kyle Carter.
    p. cm. — (The Performers discovery library)
    Includes index.
    ISBN 1-57103-066-2
    1. Circus performers—Juvenile literature. 2. Circus—United
States—Juvenile literature. [1. Circus performers. 2. Vocational
guidance. 3. Occupations.] I. Title. II. Series.
GV1817.C37   1994
791.3—dc20
                                                    94-12385
                                                       CIP
                                                        AC

Printed in the USA

TABLE OF CONTENTS

CIRCUS PERFORMERS

Circus performers are the talented people who appear in circus acts. They travel from place to place with circuses. At show time, each performer has a special act. Some circus stars are talented enough to appear in several acts.

Circus performers have entertained American circus fans for more than 200 years. In 1793 John Bill Ricketts began the first circus in America in Philadelphia, Pennsylvania.

A circus juggler performs in front of an audience in the circus tent

KINDS OF CIRCUS PERFORMERS

Each circus is a **variety** show — it has several different kinds of acts. Each act, or performance, depends on special talents.

The largest circuses, such as the Ringling Brothers and Barnum and Bailey Circus and the Clyde Beatty-Cole Brothers Circus, have the greatest number of acts and performers. They have **trapeze** artists, wild **animal trainers,** acrobats, horseback riders, clowns, jugglers, cyclists and other performers.

6 *Elephants parade in a performance with the Clyde Beatty-Cole Brothers Circus*

LEARNING TO BE A CIRCUS PERFORMER

Many people who join circuses are the sons and daughters of circus performers. They learn circus skills from their parents.

Other people go to special schools to learn circus skills. An example is the Sailor Circus in Sarasota, Florida. By working at the Sailor Circus, talented young people learn and perform circus acts.

An elephant trainer coaches a young rider to "climb aboard"

PRACTICE MAKES PERFECT

Many circus people perform in dangerous acts. Some of them work on wires and swings that are high above the ground. Other performers work with large animals — horses, elephants and bears. A few performers — the big cat trainers — climb into cages with tigers and lions!

Circus performers want to be both entertaining and safe. They practice each day to stay strong and "sharp." Animal trainers work with their animals each day, too.

Climbing into a cage with
500-pound lions is dangerous work

A circus performer swings from cords high above the ground

Most circus animals travel and live in vans

COSTUMES AND MAKEUP

Dazzling colors have always been part of the American circus. Cages, posters and wagons are painted in bright blues, reds, yellows and greens.

Circus performers add color by wearing bright costumes and makeup. Long before show time, clowns begin to carefully paint their faces with bright, bold colors. Women often wear feathery headbands.

14

A clown puts on makeup before the big show starts

ON THE CIRCUS ROAD

Circus performers travel from seven to 10 months each year. Large circuses may spend several days in one city. Smaller circuses move from one town to another almost every day.

Many American circuses travel by truck. The Ringling Brothers and Barnum and Bailey Circus still travels by train, and visits about 45 cities.

Circus performers don't live in hotels. They live in their travel trailers or train cars. After the tour season, most circuses spend the winter months in Florida.

Today, most circus performers travel by truck and van

THE CIRCUS PERFORMER'S WORKPLACE

Circus performers work in huge tents or indoor **arenas.** Arenas are large, open areas where thousands of people sit around an open floor.

Circus workers called **roustabouts** set up circus tents and take them down each time the circus travels. The Clyde Beatty-Cole Brothers Circus moves its tent about 100 times during its eight-month tour.

The ringmaster introduces the next act inside the Roberts Brothers Circus tent

ONSTAGE

Inside the tent or arena, the circus sets up large "rings." The big circuses may have acts performing in three different rings at the same time.

The ring is the circus performer's stage. It is the place where he or she performs in front of hundreds, or even thousands, of people.

Each act is introduced by the circus ringmaster. During the act, a band plays, adding to the excitement of the show.

A trapeze artist swings high above the ring at the Circus World Museum in Baraboo, Wisconsin

CAREERS FOR CIRCUS PERFORMERS

The life of a circus performer is difficult. They travel far and often. They live in trailers and train cars during their travels. Many people who begin circus careers quit because there is so much traveling and because their "homes" are so small.

Few jobs are available for people who would like to be circus performers. Over the years, the number of circuses in the United States has shrunk to 40.

Glossary

animal trainer (AN uh mul TRAY ner) — someone who teaches animals to perform certain tricks or motions

arena (uh REE nuh) — an enclosed area where performers entertain the public

roustabout (ROU stuh bout) — a circus worker who, among other jobs, sets up and takes down circus tents

trapeze (trah PEEZ) — a swing made of a short bar and held up by two ropes of equal length

variety (va RI eh tee) — having many different types or kinds